DARE WORKBOOK

Barry McDonagh

ILLUSTRATED BY TATYANA FEENEY

BMD PUBLISHING

DARE WORKBOOK

Barry McDonagh

ILLUSTRATED BY TATYANA FEENEY

Dedicated to all the brave people around the world who DARE.

Introduction

A SHORT STORY ABOUT ANXIETY

→

DAN HAD BEEN WORKING HARD
FOR MONTHS AT HIS NEW JOB.

HE WAS **STRESSED**
AND NOT SLEEPING WELL.

ONE MORNING AS HE RODE THE
ELEVATOR TO THE TOP FLOOR.

HE BECAME **OVERWHELMED**
WITH ANXIETY.

HIS HEART STARTED POUNDING HARD, HE FELT DIZZY AND COULD NOT CATCH HIS BREATH.

HE MADE IT TO HIS OFFICE AND TRIED TO **FORGET** WHAT JUST HAPPENED.

BUT...

2 DAYS LATER, THE SAME THING
HAPPENED AGAIN WHILE QUEUING TO
BUY SOME SHOPPING!

NOW HE BEGAN TO **REALLY FEAR**
SOMETHING WAS **SERIOUSLY WRONG**
WITH HIM.

TIGHT CHEST

HE STARTED TO HAVE A TON OF
BIZARRE SENSATIONS.

HE GOT ALL THE TESTS AND CHECK UPS
HE COULD AND THE DOCTOR TOLD HIM,

IT WAS 'JUST' ANXIETY.

FOR THE NEXT FEW WEEKS HE STARTED
AVOIDING ANYTHING HE THOUGHT
WOULD TRIGGER HIS ANXIETY.

HE DROVE THE **LONG** WAY TO WORK
INSTEAD OF TAKING THE BRIDGE.

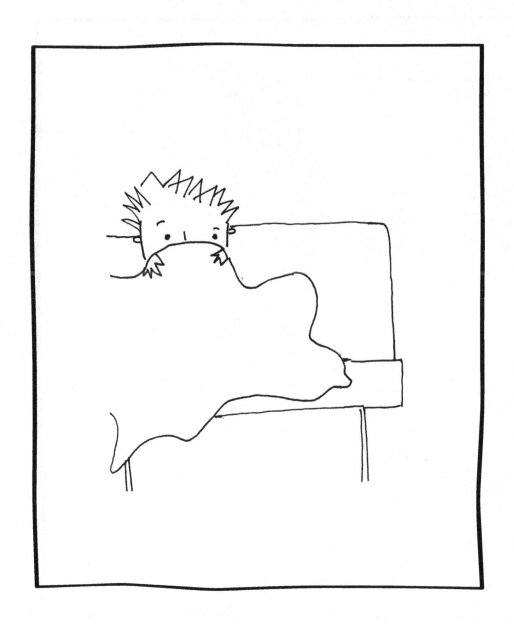

HE ORDERED ALL HiS GROCERiES ONLiNE.

HE STOPPED GOING OUT WITH FRIENDS IN CASE THEY **SUSPECTED** SOMETHING WAS **WRONG WITH HIM.**

HE STARTED HAVING **STRANGE** THOUGHTS
AND DID NOT FEEL LIKE HIMSELF AT ALL.

ANXIETY WAS NOW LIVING
WITH DAN 24/7.

OF COURSE DAN **FOUGHT HARD.**

TRIED TO GET RID OF HIS
ANXIETY AS BEST HE COULD.

BUT IT ONLY SEEMED TO MAKE
HIS ANXIETY WORSE.

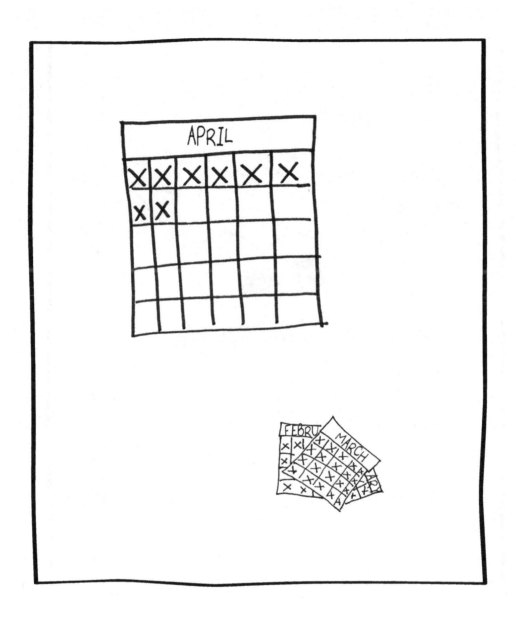

AFTER **MONTHS** OF LIVING WITH ANXIETY,

DAN DECIDED HE NEEDED **REAL** HELP.

HE WENT TO SEE A THERAPIST.

SHE TOLD HIM THAT THE **ONLY WAY**
TO GET RID OF HIS ANXIETY WAS
TO **STOP FIGHTING IT.**

SHE EXPLAINED THAT HE NEEDED TO STOP
SEEING THE ANXIETY AS A THREAT, BUT
RATHER AN **OVERPROTECTIVE** FRIEND
WHO WAS JUST TRYING TO KEEP HIM SAFE.

HE NEEDED TO BE ACCEPTING OF THE
ANXIETY AND EVEN <u>INVITE IT</u> TO STAY.
THAT WAS THE ONLY WAY IT WAS
GOING TO LEAVE.

WHEN DAN GOT HOME HE DECIDED TO GIVE IT
A TRY AS HE HAD NOTHING TO LOSE. HE WAS
NOT GOING TO FIGHT HIS ANXIETY ANYMORE.

HE **INVITED IT** TO SPEND SOME TIME WITH HIM. IN THE BEGINNING, IF HE WAS HONEST, THIS DIDN'T WORK **EXACTLY** TO PLAN.

DAN TOOK THE ANXIETY
EVERYWHERE WITH HIM.

INSTEAD OF DREADING IT
HE INVITED IT ALONG!

THEY WENT SHOPPING,

AND EVEN TO THE CINEMA.

DAN PUSHED THROUGH HIS FEARS AND STEPPED OUTSIDE HIS **COMFORT ZONE** EVERYDAY. HE USED THE **DARE** **RESPONSE** TO HELP HIM.

HE **DEFUSED** THE ANXIOUS RAMBLINGS
WITH A STRONG 'SO WHAT' OR 'WHATEVER'!

HE THEN DROPPED THE RESISTANCE AND **ALLOWED** THE ANXIETY TO BE PRESENT.

WHEN THE ANXIETY THEN PEAKED INTO
HIGH ANXIETY AS iT USUALLY DiD,
HE WOULD **RUN TOWARDS** iT.

DAN ALSO MADE SOME IMPORTANT
LIFESTYLE CHANGES HIS THERAPIST
RECOMMENDED.

HE CUT OUT COFFEE AND ALCOHOL
AND STARTED EXERCISING MORE THAN
EVER BEFORE.

AFTER LOTS OF PRACTICE AND A FEW
SETBACKS, DAN WOKE ONE MORNING TO
FIND HIS ANXIETY WAS... GONE!

JUST LIKE THAT.
NO GOODBYES, JUST A SHORT NOTE.

AFTER THAT DAN REALLY GOT HIS OLD
CAREFREE LIFE BACK. HE **NO LONGER**
SECOND GUESSED HIS EVERY STEP.

HE DID THINGS WITH A SENSE OF FREEDOM AGAIN. IN FACT, DAN FELT STRONGER AND **MORE RESILIENT** BECAUSE OF THE EXPERIENCE.

ON OCCASION ANXIETY COMES BACK TO
VISIT HIM. USUALLY IF HE IS STRESSED OR
EXHAUSTED. BUT ANXIETY JUST DOES
NOT HAVE THE TEETH IT USED TO. IT'S
JUST NORMAL EVERYDAY ANXIETY.

IF DAN HAS A BIG THING COMING UP LIKE A
WORK PRESENTATION, HE EXPECTS THE ANXIETY
TO SHOW UP. HE USES HIS DARE STEPS AND
THAT MAKES IT ALL THE EASIER.

A YEAR LATER, ANXIETY SHOWED UP ON DAN'S
HOLIDAY WHILE IN THE CARIBBEAN, BECAUSE HE
WAS ANXIOUS ABOUT BEING FAR FROM HOME.

BUT AFTER JUST ONE DAY ANXIETY
LEFT HIM AGAIN. THERE WAS JUST NOT
ENOUGH STIMULATION.

DAN DOESN'T MISS HIS ANXIETY, BUT HE DOES APPRECIATE HOW THE EXPERIENCE HAS TAUGHT HIM TO BE **MORE CONFIDENT** AND **UNDERSTANDING** OF OTHERS.

THE
END

ARE YOU READY

TO DARE?

This workbook is divided into <u>4 Parts</u>. Each part builds upon the last to move you closer to a FULL RECOVERY from anxiety.

This workbook is designed to be written in so please scribble, write and draw all over it. Keep it like a private diary.

Time to get started
(I don't see a pen in your hand!)

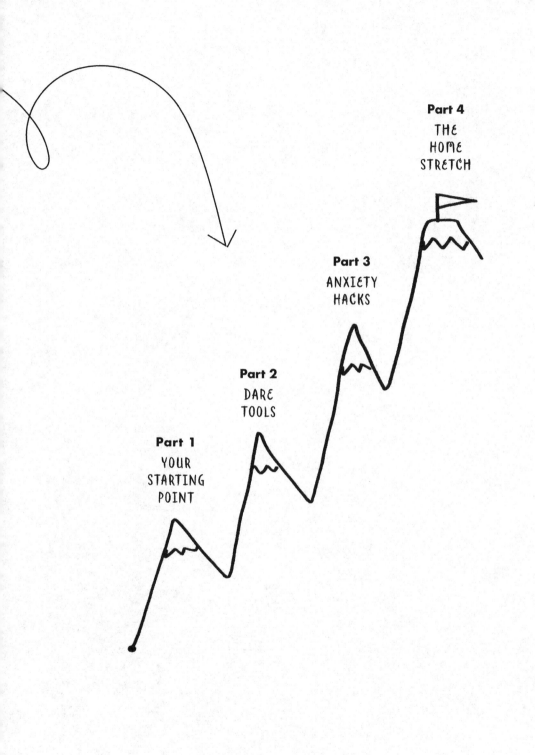

Part 1
YOUR
STARTING
POINT

Part 2
DARE
TOOLS

Part 3
ANXIETY
HACKS

Part 4
THE
HOME
STRETCH

Part 1

YOUR STARTING POINT

→

Here you get AN OVERVIEW of how anxiety has been holding you back. You will also clarify the reason WHY you must now OVERCOME IT!

Your WHY will become the driving force of your recovery.

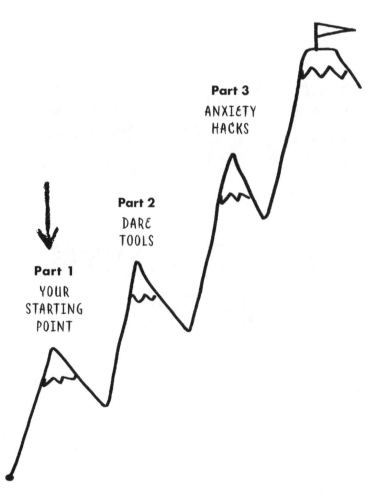

Part 4
THE
HOME
STRETCH

Part 3
ANXIETY
HACKS

Part 2
DARE
TOOLS

Part 1
YOUR
STARTING
POINT

DO YOU LIVE YOUR LIFE
WITHIN A **SAFE ZONE?**

WRITE WHAT IS OUTSIDE
THIS ZONE.

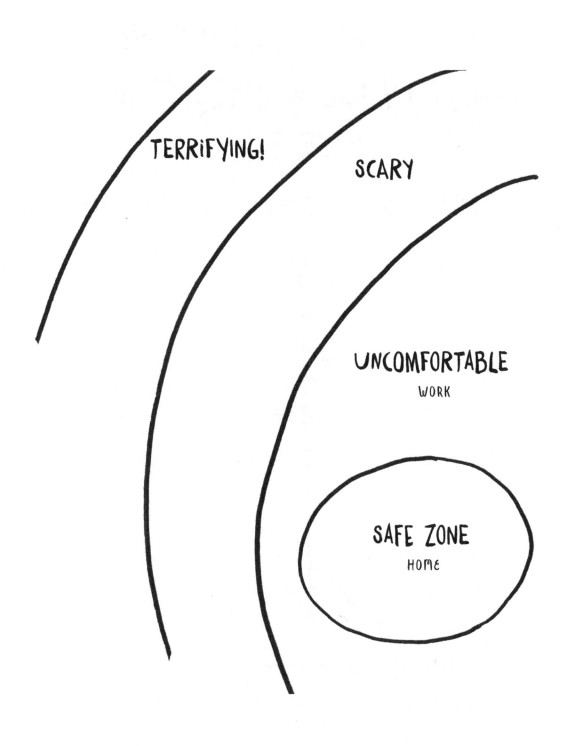

DRAW A LINE INDICATING HOW ANXIETY HAS MANIFESTED IN YOUR LIFE.

(HERE IS AN EXAMPLE WITH YEARS FILLED IN)

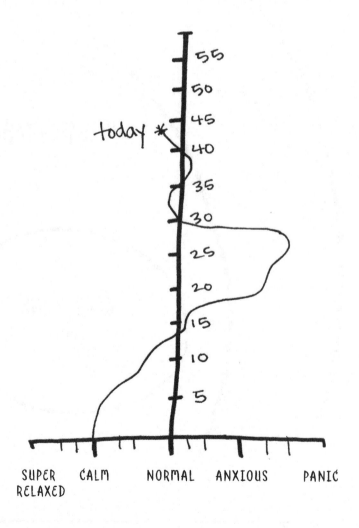

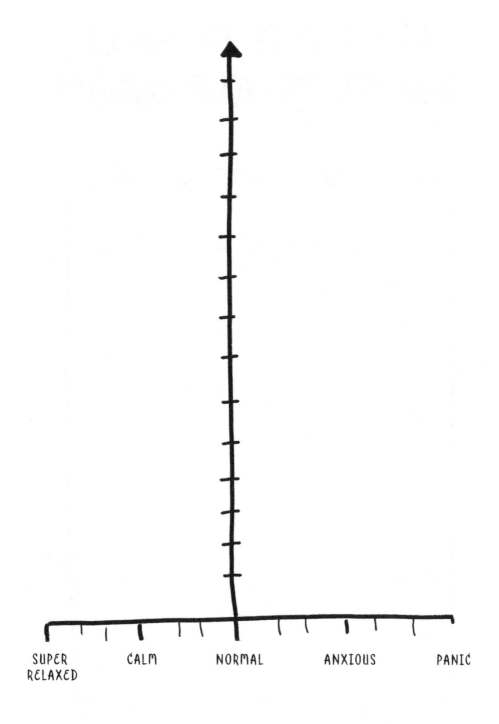

SUPER
RELAXED   CALM   NORMAL   ANXIOUS   PANIC

DO A LIST OF THE THINGS THAT TRIGGER YOUR ANXIETY

1. DRIVING IN TRAFFIC

2. POUNDING HEART

NOW DO A LIST OF WHY YOU NEED TO OVERCOME THIS

1. SO I CAN DRIVE WITH COMFORT ANYWHERE

2. SO I CAN FEEL SAFE IN MY BODY

WHAT AREAS OF YOUR LIFE ARE MOST AFFECTED BY ANXIETY?

SCORE THE BOXES BELOW FROM 0-10,
WHERE 0 IS LEAST AFFECTED AND 10 IS THE MOST.

AN EXAMPLE IS SHOWN BELOW:

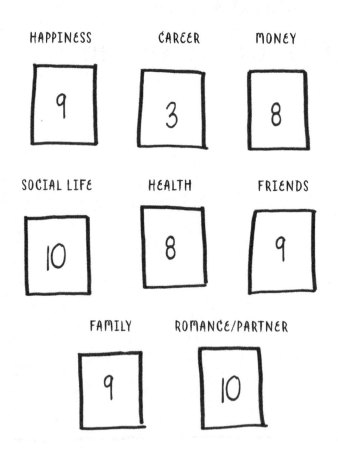

HAPPINESS   CAREER   MONEY
9   3   8

SOCIAL LIFE HEALTH   FRIENDS
10   8   9

FAMILY   ROMANCE/PARTNER
9   10

YOUR TURN:

HAPPINESS

CAREER

MONEY

SOCIAL LIFE

HEALTH

FRIENDS

FAMILY

ROMANCE/PARTNER

A 90-YEAR HUMAN
LIFE IN YEARS

0 0 0 0 0 0 0 0 0 0

0 0 0 0 0 0 0 0 0 0

0 0 0 0 0 0 0 0 0 0   30

0 0 0 0 0 0 0 0 0 0

0 0 0 0 0 0 0 0 0 0

0 0 0 0 0 0 0 0 0 0   60

0 0 0 0 0 0 0 0 0 0

0 0 0 0 0 0 0 0 0 0

0 0 0 0 0 0 0 0 0 0 ← 90

MARK WHERE YOU ARE ON THE CHART
RIGHT NOW. HOW MANY YEARS HAVE YOU
STRUGGLED WITH ANXIETY?

TIME is YOUR MOST PRECIOUS RESOURCE. DON'T LET ANXIETY STEAL ANYMORE OF IT FROM YOU!

WHAT DO YOU WANT TO DO WITH YOUR LIFE BEFORE YOU KICK THE BUCKET?

WRITE YOUR BUCKET LIST BELOW:

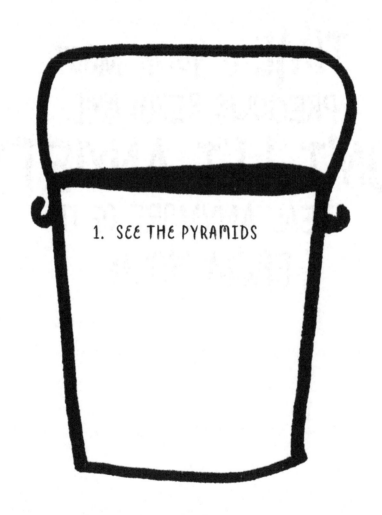

1. SEE THE PYRAMIDS

WHAT ARE THE THREE MOST IMPORTANT REASONS FOR YOU TO OVERCOME YOUR ANXIETY PROBLEMS?

1. ....

2. ....

3. ....

*KEEP THESE IN MIND ANYTIME YOU FEEL LIKE GIVING UP.

IF ANXIETY WAS NOT A PROBLEM, HOW WOULD YOUR LIFE LOOK?

YOU CAN START TO TRUST THAT IT'S GOING TO BE OKAY!

YOU WILL GET THROUGH THIS.

IN FACT, NOT ONLY ARE YOU
GOING TO GET THROUGH THIS,
BUT YOU CAN JOURNEY TO
A PLACE OF FULL RECOVERY
AND BECOME A **STRONGER**
PERSON BECAUSE OF IT.

THE GIFT IS IN THE WOUND.

Part 2

DARE
TOOLS

→

Part 1 has been about identifying how anxiety shows up in your life, as well as clarifying your MAIN REASONS TO OVERCOME IT.

Next you are going to start implementing DARE!

READY?

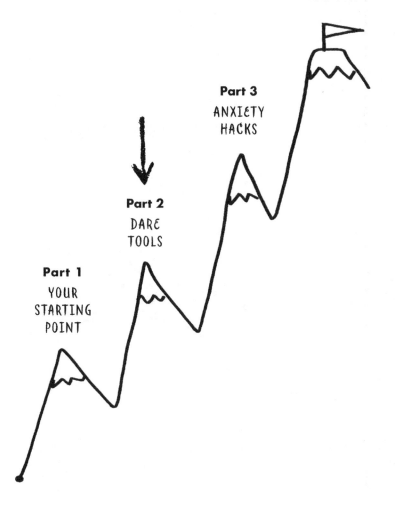

Part 4
THE
HOME
STRETCH

Part 3
ANXIETY
HACKS

Part 2
DARE
TOOLS

Part 1
YOUR
STARTING
POINT

DARE - RIDING THE WAVE OF ANXIETY

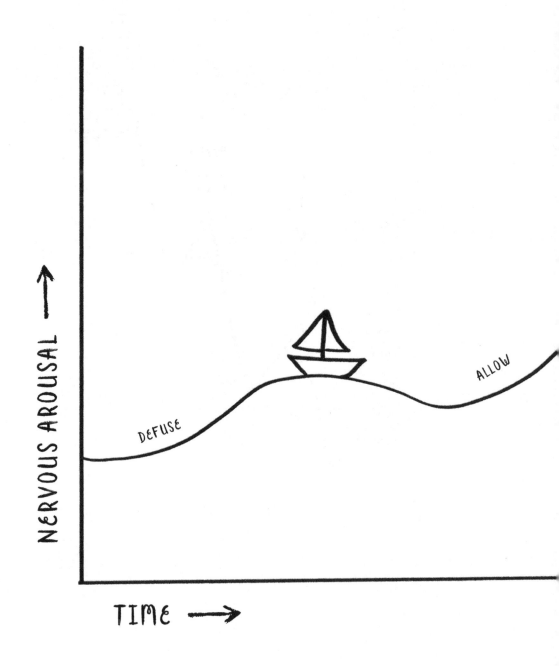

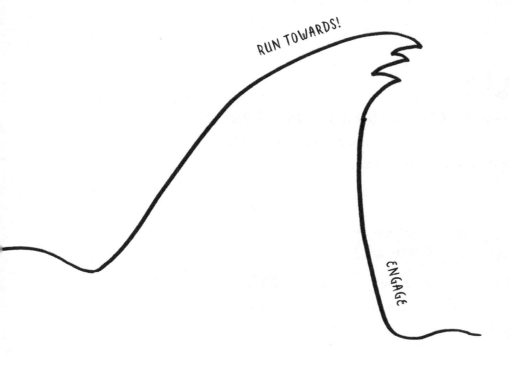

RUN TOWARDS!

ENGAGE

D EFUSE

Neutralize the fear as it arises. Replace scary 'what if' thoughts with a dismissive 'SO WHAT' or 'WHATEVER'. You can handle this no matter what happens.

A LLOW

Tell yourself, 'I ACCEPT AND ALLOW THIS ANXIOUS FEELING'. Welcome the anxiety as a protective friend. Resisting it only fuels the fear.

R UN TOWARDS

Demand more of the anxiety. 'I AM EXCITED BY THIS FEELING.' 'Bring it on, I want more!!!', 'Is that all you've got?'

E NGAGE

Move your attention to something that FULLY ENGAGES YOU. For example, reading, talking or work. When your mind STRAYS, bring your focus back to your activity.

THESE ARE YOUR STEPS TO FREEDOM

What follows are exercises to help you practice each of the steps in DARE. The more you practice each step, the faster your recovery will be.

BUT...

BEFORE YOU BEGIN YOU
NEED A VISUAL PICTURE OF
YOUR ANXIETY IN YOUR HEAD

DRAW A CARTOON VERSION OF
YOUR ANXIETY HERE

NAME: _____

THE DARE RESPONSE

You do not break free from anxiety by trying to be calm. You BREAK FREE BY ACTING BRAVELY. That bravery overrides your fear because no matter where you are or what you are feeling, you know deep down that you can handle it!

The DARE Response teaches you to have a NEW BRAVE RELATIONSHIP with your anxiety. The unusual thing about The DARE Response is that it's not designed to get rid of your anxiety; it's DESIGNED TO GET RID OF YOUR FEAR OF THE ANXIETY. It's your resistance to and struggle with anxiety that keeps you trapped. A bit like quicksand, the more you struggle, the deeper you sink. When you employ The DARE Response, your anxious mind is taken out of the way, allowing you to connect back with life again.

As strange as it sounds, THE GREATEST OBSTACLE TO HEALING YOUR ANXIETY IS YOU. You're the cure. Your body wants to heal your anxiety as much as you do. All you need to learn is a new and better response.

The DARE Response is made up of four brave steps:

DEFUSE

ALLOW

RUN TOWARDS &

ENGAGE

SMILE
AT THE ANXIOUS
'WHAT IF'S' IN
YOUR MIND

WHATEVER!

DARE: DEFUSE

The very first step of DARE is the letter 'D' and it stands for DEFUSE. This step retrains how you immediately respond to anxiety. It's your first point of contact with the anxiety, and it's a very quick and easy step to implement. You want to *defuse* the buildup of anxious energy by dismissing the fearful 'what if' thoughts that crowd your mind as soon as you start to feel anxious. Those what if's might be:

- What if my heart doesn't stop pounding?
- What if I have a panic attack here in the car?
- What if I faint in public? Who will help me?
- What if my mind never stops obsessing with these thoughts?

I bet you already know what your own particular what if thoughts are. The ones that really make you afraid. You defuse those 'what if' thoughts by responding to them with a strong 'SO WHAT' or 'WHATEVER' type response. For example:

WHAT IF MY HEART DOESN'T STOP POUNDING?

SO WHAT! My heart's an incredibly strong muscle. This is nothing more than a light workout for it.

WHAT IF I HAVE A PANIC ATTACK HERE IN THE CAR?

SO WHAT! I'll pull over and get through it like I've always done in the past.

WHAT IF I FAINT IN PUBLIC? WHO WILL HELP ME?

SO WHAT! If I faint, I faint. Someone will help me, and in two minutes I'll be conscious again.

WHAT IF MY MIND NEVER STOPS OBSESSING WITH THESE THOUGHTS?

SO WHAT! Thoughts are just thoughts and can't harm me. Eventually my anxious mind will settle, and the thoughts will dissipate.

You can make your response even more effective by using strong emotive language, something like 'Ahh who gives a ****!'

DEFUSE ALLOW RUN TOWARDS ENGAGE

DARE: DEFUSE

This new response of 'So what', 'Whatever' is such an important first step because it quickly disarms the buildup of tension and gets you moving in the same direction as the nervous arousal instead of against it. This step FLIPS THE MENTAL CONTROL BACK TO YOU making it harder for your anxiety to escalate. Be creative and have fun with this step. Come up with dismissive replies that fit your own particular sense of humor so that it feels right for you.

WHAT IF?????

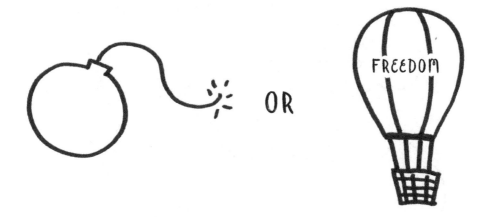

OR

FREEDOM

YOU HAVE THE POWER
TO ALWAYS CHOOSE A
BETTER RESPONSE
TO YOUR ANXIETY.

DARE: DEFUSE

WRITE ALL YOUR ANXIOUS 'WHAT IF' FEARS IN THE CLOUDS

DISMISS THEM WITH AN EMOTIONAL

'SO WHAT!' OR 'WHATEVER'.

DARE: DEFUSE

COME UP WITH YOUR FUNNIEST REPLIES TO YOUR SCARIEST 'WHAT IF'S'

WHAT IF I GET LOCKED UP?
....

WHAT IF I PASS OUT?
....

....

....

....

....

....

....

REPLY WITH:

WHATEVER! AT LEAST I WON'T HAVE TO COOK AND CLEAN ANYMORE.
....

SO WHAT! I COULD DO WITH A QUICK NAP.
....

....

....

....

....

....

DARE: DEFUSE

SORRY, YOU'RE NOT UNIQUE ☹

Your weird anxious thoughts and strange anxiety sensations are not unique to you alone. There are literally thousands of people right now with the same bizarre intrusive thoughts, the same sensation of unreality and the same anxious physical sensations. Although you might strongly disagree, your anxiety is probably as boring and predictable as everyone else's.

STRIP ANXIETY
OF ITS POWER BY
NORMALIZING IT

'SO WHAT!'
'WHATEVER'

DARE: ALLOW

The letter 'A' in Dare stands for Allow. This step is about learning to allow the anxiety to manifest in whatever way it wishes. You see when you resist anxiety, you pull against it, creating a further buildup of internal tension, making it harder to discharge. Don't pull away or fight the anxiety; that never works. TURN INTO IT, ALLOW IT, AND MOVE WITH IT.

If anxiety wants to make your throat feel tight, go ahead and let it. If it wants to make your heart pound, great. If it wants to make your mind race with wild thoughts, let it be your guest. LET YOUR BODY VIBRATE WITH THE NERVOUS AROUSAL without any hindrance so it can then start to unwind. When done correctly, this has a soothing effect on your nervous system, allowing it to desensitize from the anxious state you've been holding it in.

You can practice this step by repeating out loud or to yourself:

'I accept and allow this anxious feeling.'

'I accept and allow these anxious thoughts.'

Allowing enables you to gracefully MOVE WITH THE NERVOUS AROUSAL YOU FEEL rather than against it. So no matter what the bodily sensation or thought is that makes you anxious, you must learn to allow it to be present, and then come to accept it for what it is—nervous arousal and nothing more.

In essence, you are learning to GET COMFORTABLE WITH YOUR ANXIOUS DISCOMFORT. Once you really allow and accept it, it begins to fall away and discharge naturally. It's the paradox of healing anxiety. Accepting the discomfort in order to become free of it.

Before, you resisted each and every sensation because your anxious mind thought that was the right thing to do, but now you're LEARNING TO SIT WITH IT IN FRIENDLY CURIOSITY, allowing it to be as it is without any desire to stop or control it.

Don't get upset when anxiety shows up. Just let the anxious energy play itself out. It might calm down soon or it might stay a while. Who knows? The important thing is to not get upset or fearful about it.

HOW MUCH ANXIOUS DISCOMFORT ARE YOU WILLING TO ACCEPT EACH DAY IN ORDER TO RECOVER?

DEFUSE **ALLOW** RUN TOWARDS ENGAGE

DARE: ALLOW

LIST YOUR MOST COMMON
ANXIOUS SENSATIONS

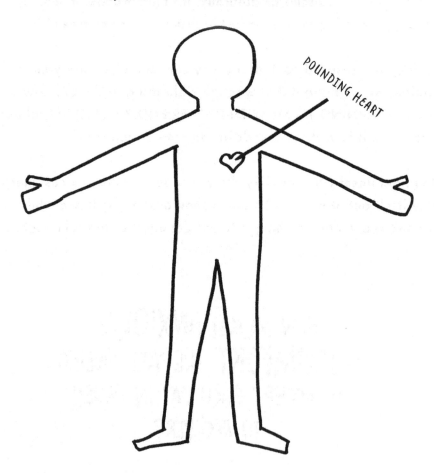

POUNDING HEART

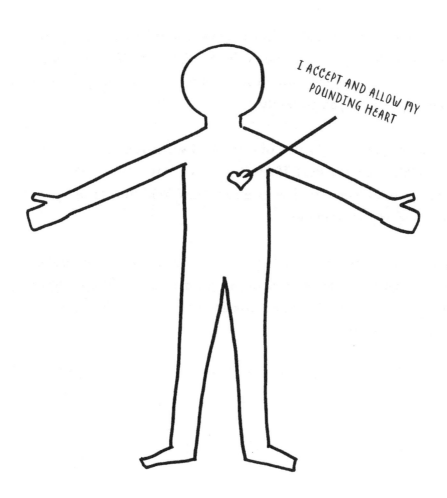

DARE: ALLOW
YOUR ANXiETY STONE

Acceptance is sometimes a hard concept to grasp so here is an exercise to help you with that step. BEGIN BY FINDING A SMALL STONE. Something that would fit comfortably in your pocket. This stone represents your anxiety.

Whenever you feel a wave of anxiety, I want you to IMAGINE ALL THAT NERVOUS ENERGY TRANSFERRING INTO THE STONE. Feel it buzzing in the stone and your body. Now hold the stone in your hand and say to yourself:

"Whatever, I accept and allow this anxious feeling. I am not going to push it away. I am embracing it, in fact I am holding it tightly in my hand and won't let it go. Anxiety you are all mine. Let's spend the day together!"

Then instead of throwing the stone into the nearest river, you are going to CARRY IT AROUND WITH YOU WHEREVER YOU GO. Hold it there in your hand as you go shopping or for a walk. Hold it as you talk to people. Hold it as you watch TV. Put the stone in your pocket (or handbag) and bring it everywhere with you. Tell it that it's welcome to stay with you. It's your new buddy. You can even draw a face on it and give it a name.

THE STONE GIVES YOU A TANGIBLE OBJECT THAT YOU CAN FEEL IN YOUR HAND to represent your thoughts and feelings. There is something about physically holding your fears and worries in your hand that creates a pleasant gap between you and it. This allows you to feel more distant and removed from your anxiety.

DARE: ALLOW

DROP THE RESISTANCE!

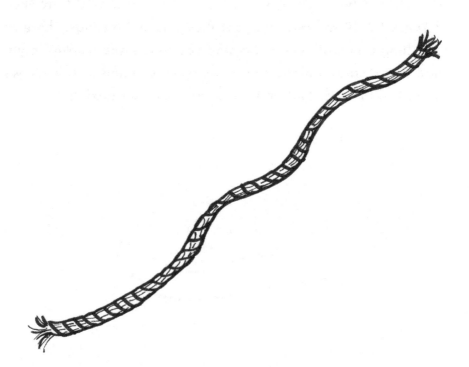

SPEND 5 MINUTES
RIGHT NOW IN TOTAL ACCEPTANCE
OF ALL THE ANXIETY YOU FEEL.

'I ACCEPT AND ALLOW THIS ANXIOUS FEELING.'

DARE: ALLOW

SYMPHONY TECHNIQUE

This exercise is very useful for the second step of DARE (Accept). It trains you to accept and flow with your anxious thoughts and sensations instead of resisting them.

You start by IMAGINING YOURSELF AS THE CONDUCTOR OF A SYMPHONY ORCHESTRA. You are going to learn how to conduct and move the stagnant anxious feelings in your body through rhythm and movement. Begin by establishing a 4/4 rhythm by counting like this:

1 and 2 and 3 and 4
1 and 2 and 3 and 4

As you count, TAP YOUR FEET ON EACH NUMBER AND MOVE YOUR HANDS as you imagine a symphony conductor would do. (If you are not alone you can do this in your imagination and just tap your feet, however it does work much better to do it physically).

1 and 2 and 3 and 4.

Now in this 4/4 time repeat the following sentence:

'I accept and allow this anxious feeling'.
1 and 2 and 3 and 4.

'I accept and allow these anxious thoughts'.
1 and 2 and 3 and 4.

Repeat this over and over and REALLY GET INTO THE SENSE OF MOVEMENT that you are creating. You are in control; you are the conductor moving the inner sensations/anxiety with the wave of your hands and the tapping of your feet.

ALLOW YOURSELF TO FEEL ALL OF THE ANXIETY IN ITS FULLEST. Stand up and move around if that helps you get more of a flow going. By allowing yourself to feel the anxiety in this way, you start to accept it. By accepting it you start to process it. There are no set rules on how long you should do this. However, you should do it for a few minutes to feel the effects.

DARE: ALLOW

MAKE FRIENDS WITH YOUR HEART

Many people who experience anxiety worry about their heart. They worry about it pounding too hard or maybe skipped heart beats. They also fear having their heart rate monitored.

Your heart's sole purpose is to keep you alive and well, also to be fair it has done a wonderful job of that to date! Your heart is not an atomic clock that must always keep perfect time. It speeds up; it slows down. Occasionally it may beat faster than usual and at other times you may notice irregular beats.

If you're anxious about your heart, you should certainly get your heart health checked out if for nothing else than to put your mind at ease, and reduce the effect of anxious 'what if' thoughts.

The following exercise is designed to help you get more comfortable with the beatings of your heart:

- Once a day place your hand on your heart and spend a moment paying full attention to every beat.
- Allow your heart to beat in whatever way it wishes, fast or slow, hard or soft. Don't try to control anything. Instead say 'I accept and allow whatever way my heart beats'.
- Finish by telling your heart how grateful you are for the incredible work it does. For the relentless way it serves to keep you alive and well!

(The same exercise can be done for breathing anxiety e.g. 'I accept and allow my tight chest').

DARE: RUN TOWARDS

'THE ONLY WAY OUT...

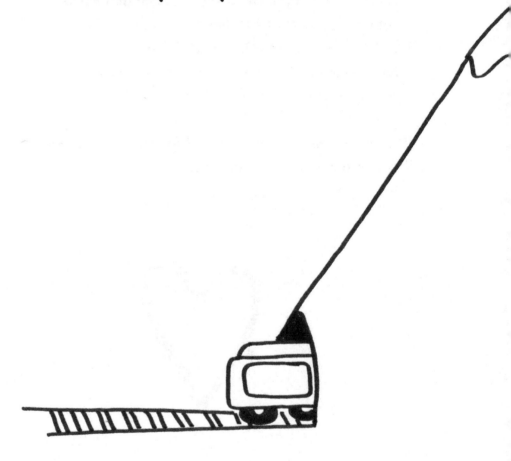

... iS THROUGH'

DARE: RUN TOWARDS

The previous two steps (Defuse and Allow) are the primary drivers that heal your anxiety. They propel you forward and often are enough to get you where you want to be. If, however, the anxiety still feels like a harmful threat hanging over you, YOU NEED TO NOW SHATTER THAT ILLUSION BY IMPLEMENTING THE THIRD STEP. The letter 'R' in DARE stands for 'run towards'.

You run towards anxiety by telling yourself YOU FEEL EXCITED BY ALL THIS NERVOUS AROUSAL AND DEMAND MORE OF IT! Anxiety is nothing more than a wave of energy flowing through your body. THIS ENERGY WILL NOT HURT YOU. It's your interpretation of this heightened energy that causes the problem and traps you in the vicious cycle of fearing fear. So tell yourself *'I'm excited by this feeling! Give me more. Bring it on!'*

Talk to your anxiety and demand that it increase the intensity of the bodily sensations that scare you. For example, if your heart's pounding fast, you say: *'Okay, anxiety, that's good, but can you make my heart pound even faster!?'* You feel you can't catch your breath, so you say: *'Come on anxiety make my throat and chest feel even tighter. Let's have more of this!'* *'I am starting to feel a bit dizzy, but I wonder how dizzy I can get? Can't you make me dizzier? Is that the best you can do?'*

Let your anxiety know you're making a firm request, that you want to experience the very worst it can throw at you. Anxiety tries to convince you that you're in danger, but that's SIMPLY NOT TRUE— SO YOU CALL ITS BLUFF.

In the beginning, you may have to FAKE IT TILL YOU MAKE IT. That means that initially you'll find it hard to really run toward it and believe you're excited rather than scared, but with regular practice, the sensations that terrify you (e.g., a pounding heart, sweating palms, palpitations, dizziness, shortness of breath, queasy stomach) all become just that—sensations and nothing more.

Now YOU chase the anxiety, -running after it, getting excited and demanding that it show you more! You become the hunter not the hunted! This brave new mindset moves you out of feeling like a victim and into a state of empowerment.

DARE: RUN TOWARDS

WHAT SITUATIONS MAKE YOU REALLY ANXIOUS?

DRIVING IN TRAFFIC
....

....

....

....

....

....

....

WRITE OUT YOUR NEW RUN TOWARDS RESPONSE FOR EACH SITUATION.
(IN THE PRESENT TENSE)

'I AM EXCITED TO BE DRIVING. BRING IT ON!'

....

....

....

....

....

....

....

DARE: RUN TOWARDS
21 SECOND COUNTDOWN

The 21 Second Countdown is a useful 'run towards' exercise to help stop a panic attack quickly. Here is how it works:

When you feel your anxiety tip over into a sense of panic, tell your anxiety that it has 21 seconds to initiate the panic attack that it threatens. TWENTY-ONE SECONDS TO DO ITS WORST! You are not just telling your anxiety this but demanding it. Twenty-one seconds to get as bad as it is going to get, BUT IF AFTER 21 SECONDS NOTHING HAS HAPPENED, IT MUST STOP MAKING EMPTY THREATS.

Whatever the issue is that you fear, it must happen within that 21 second time frame.
- If your heart is going to explode, then it has 21 seconds to do so.
- If you are going to stop breathing, then you have 21 seconds to do so.
- If you are going to faint—21 seconds! But absolutely no more time than that.

By setting a specific time frame YOU TURN THE TABLE AND ESTABLISH CLEAR BOUNDARIES OF CONTROL. In short, you call panic's bluff. If it were a poker game, you would be asking panic to show its hand. You say to yourself *'I am not going to waste any more time and energy worrying about this. I've had enough. I am going to be generous and give my anxiety 21 seconds to get as bad as it's going to get, but if after 21 seconds are up and nothing has happened, then sorry, but the opportunity has officially passed.'*

NOW START COUNTING DOWN FROM 21 – but nice and slowly, don't rattle it off as fast as you can. Really tease it out like you did when you were a child playing a game and you never wanted to reach zero. Teasing it out is key because it allows you to feel generous; you are really giving your anxiety every chance possible to do its worst. So when you get around number 5, break the last few into fractions →

21 SECOND COUNTDOWN
(CONTINUED)

5...........................

4...........................

3............................

2...AND THREE QUARTERS...

2...AND HALF...............

2...........................

1...AND THREE QUARTERS... (LAST CHANCE)

1...AND A HALF.............. (I REALLY CAN'T WAIT ANY

LONGER)

1...........................

0

Sorry, too late, we've run out of time. This countdown works because it places you in charge of the nervous arousal that you feel. It helps you to re-establish control. You learn to trust that there is no threat and that you are safe. Incredibly, you have demanded that a panic attack should happen, and it did not. You demanded that the sensations you feared most should do their worst, and... nothing. You are still alive and well and in one piece.

DARE: RUN TOWARDS

IF YOU ARE GOING TO
HAVE A PANIC ATTACK,
WHY NOT HAVE ONE OUT
LIVING LIFE SOMEPLACE
FUN INSTEAD OF ALWAYS
AT HOME!

DARE TO
BRING IT ON!

DARE: RUN TOWARDS
BURN IT OFF!

When you are in a heightened state of anxiety or panic, adrenaline and cortisol are released as your body is priming itself to fight or flee. These stress hormones can make your body feel very jittery and on edge for quite some time. Here is a PHYSICAL EXERCISE you can do during the 3rd step of DARE (Run Towards) to help you burn off this nervous energy faster.

1. When a panic attack kicks in, you move to the third step of Dare - 'Get excited by the arousal and DEMAND MORE OF IT'.

2. As you do this, I want you to CLASP YOUR HAND TOGETHER AND CONTRACT ALL THE MUSCLES in your body for 5 seconds and then rest for 10 seconds.

3. Do FIVE repetitions of this. Contract all muscles for 5 seconds and then rest for 10 seconds. Contract and release. Contract and release. This means you are contracting your calf muscles, thighs, buttocks, stomach, chest, arms and hands. You can even clench your jaw if you want. The more muscles you contract the better.

Contracting muscles sends a message to your amygdala that you are fleeing the threat and that it can now turn off the stress response. IT'S LIKE A 'FAKE FLEE' SIGNAL. The contractions also help to burn off the excessive adrenaline and nervous energy that you feel.

You could of course run on the spot which would be even better but that's not always easy to do if you are in the post office or on an airplane!

DARE: RUN TOWARDS
IN CASE OF EMERGENCY

If in a moment of extreme panic you forget what steps to take, remind yourself of this:

- No matter how unpleasant the sensations feel, YOU ARE NOT IN ANY DANGER. This will soon pass. You are safe!

- You have a 100% SUCCESS RATE for surviving panic attacks.

- Don't worry about embarrassing yourself. NO ONE IS LOOKING AT YOU. More likely than not, no one has any idea what's going on with you unless you tell them so.

- Lastly, in your bravest voice say to yourself. 'I AM EXCITED BY THIS FEELING. BRING IT ON!' (It's ok to be scared, fake it till you make it.)

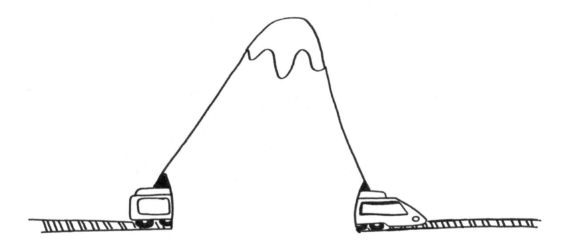

DEFUSE   ALLOW   RUN TOWARDS   ENGAGE

BE THE HUNTER...

...NOT THE HUNTED

DARE: ENGAGE

ANXIETY TAKES YOU OUT OF LIFE

DARE PLACES YOU RIGHT BACK IN IT!

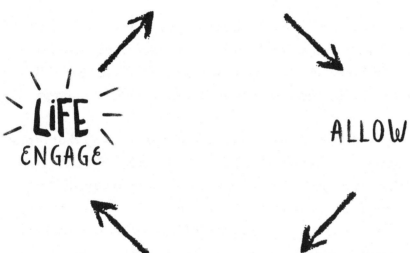

DARE: ENGAGE

Your anxious mind will always look for ways to hook you back into a state of worry and fear. In order to avoid this, you need to ENGAGE WITH SOMETHING THAT TAKES UP YOUR FULL ATTENTION. The fourth step in The DARE Response, the 'E' of DARE is *engage*.

This final step entails occupying yourself with an activity that really engages your mind, ANYTHING AT ALL THAT TAKES UP YOUR FULL ATTENTION, such as going for a walk, focusing on a specific task at work, or having a conversation with someone in person or on the phone. Doing this keeps you in a STATE OF FLOW and prevents you from getting hooked back into the anxiety loop again.

Don't get upset if the anxiety keeps intruding. It will — that's often inevitable. So when it does, just KEEP GENTLY PLACING YOUR ATTENTION BACK ON WHAT YOU WERE ENGAGED WITH. Carry on in the full knowledge that you're doing everything right and that your new approach is working in the background as you engage with other activities.

This last step of the DARE Response is short but crucial as it completes the cycle from start to finish. Anxiety takes you out of life. THIS FINAL LAST STEP PLACES YOU RIGHT BACK INTO IT. Back into the present moment, happily engaged with life and not caught up worrying about your fear and anxiety.

WRITE DOWN ALL THE THINGS YOU
REALLY LIKE DOING
THAT ENGAGE YOU

AT HOME:

....

....

....

AT WORK:

....

....

....

WITH FRIENDS:

....

....

....

RANDOM THINGS:

....

....

....

DEFUSE   ALLOW   RUN TOWARDS   ENGAGE

DARE: ENGAGE

COLOUR IN THE DRAWING BELOW. AS YOU ENGAGE
WITH THE COLOURING, ALLOW ANXIETY TO BE **FULLY**
PRESENT WITH YOU. DO NOT PUSH IT AWAY.

DARE: ENGAGE

NEXT TIME YOU EAT, BE FULLY PRESENT.
CHEW **SLOWLY**.

TASTE EVERY BITE.
SMELL ALL THE AROMAS.

STOP AND NOTICE SOME
OF THE SOUNDS AROUND YOU
RIGHT NOW.

HOW MANY DIFFERENT
SOUNDS CAN YOU IDENTIFY?
LET SOUNDS ANCHOR YOU INTO THE
PRESENT MOMENT.

DARE: ENGAGE

GO FOR A WALK
OUTSIDE IN NATURE

FEEL THE GROUND
BENEATH YOUR FEET

FEEL THE WIND
ON YOUR FACE

FEEL YOUR BODY
IN MOTION

USE ALL YOUR SENSES AND
WHEN ANXIETY TRIES TO GET YOUR
ATTENTION, GENTLY BRING YOUR
FOCUS BACK TO THE WALK

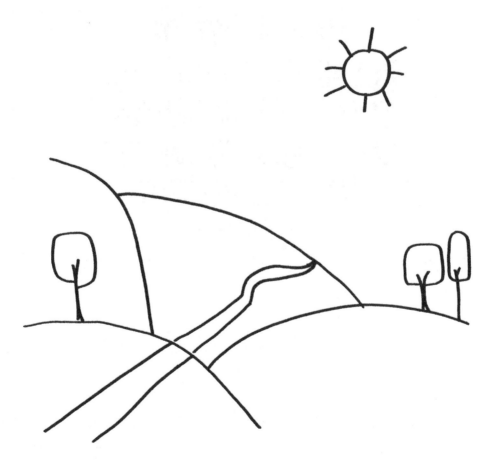

DARE: ENGAGE

MAKE A LIST OF
PLEASANT THINGS THAT
ENGAGE YOUR SENSES.
USE THESE TO ANCHOR
INTO THE PRESENT
MOMENT:

SMELL

FRESH CUT GRASS

....

....

....

SOUND

BIRDS SINGING

....

....

....

TASTE

RIPE MANGOES

....

....

....

TOUCH

BUBBLE WRAP

....

....

....

DEFUSE   ALLOW   RUN TOWARDS   ENGAGE

DARE: ENGAGE

ANXIETY WILL TRY TO HOOK YOU BACK IN.

IF YOU GET HOOKED, SMILE AT THE THOUGHT AND BRING YOUR FOCUS BACK TO THE PRESENT MOMENT.

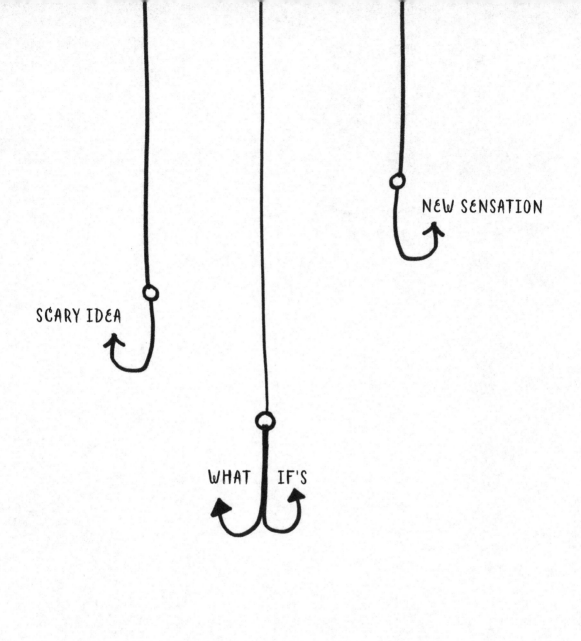

Part 3
- - - - - - - -

ANXIETY HACKS →

Use the
following exercises
to SUPERCHARGE
your recovery!

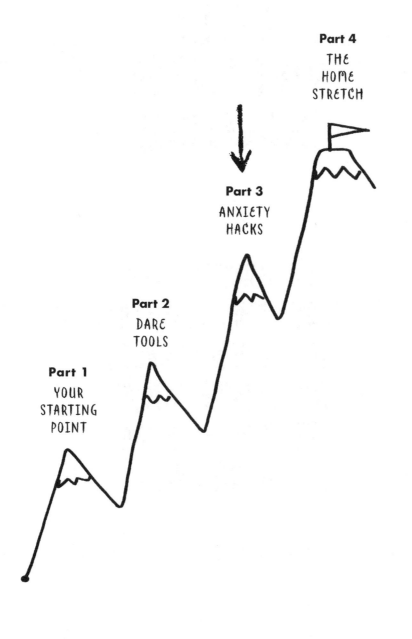

Part 4
THE
HOME
STRETCH

Part 3
ANXIETY
HACKS

Part 2
DARE
TOOLS

Part 1
YOUR
STARTING
POINT

DAILY WELLNESS ROUTINE

COMBINED WITH DARE, THIS ROUTINE WILL DRAMATICALLY ACCELERATE YOUR RECOVERY FROM ANXIETY:

1. When you wake in the morning do some **LIGHT STRETCHING** to get out of your head and into a state of flow.

2. During your morning shower **TURN THE WATER ICE COLD** and shower for 30 seconds. This is to stimulate the release of endorphins and shake off anxious fog.

3. Eat a **HEALTHY BREAKFAST** and take a magnesium supplement (250–300mg daily).

4. Ensure you drink at least **8 GLASSES OF FRESH WATER** throughout the day. (No caffeine or alcohol and keep sugar to a minimum).

5. Do **20–30 MINUTES OF AEROBIC EXERCISE** daily and sustain for as many days as possible.

6. Ensure you get at least **8 HOURS SLEEP PER NIGHT.** (Refrain from watching news or screen time before bed, instead read light fiction or journal about the things you are grateful for that day).

GOOD SLEEP HABITS

1. Prepare for a good night's sleep by taking a MAGNESIUM SUPPLEMENT or herbal tea (Chamomile/Valerian) before bed.

2. No SCREEN TIME (TV/phone) an hour before bed. Wind down with some light fiction.

3. Insomnia is most often caused by the fear of not being able to sleep. To break the cycle of insomnia STOP TRYING SO HARD TO SLEEP. Approach each night as an opportunity to sleep; not a given. In fact, you can experiment with trying your best to stay awake for as long as you can. (This removes the constant pressure you're placing yourself under to sleep).

4. If your mind is racing with anxious thoughts go to another room and **WRITE YOUR WORRIES OUT ON PAPER**. Keep writing them out over and over until you feel tired or very bored with the exercise, then return to bed.

5. Set **AN ALARM** but don't constantly check the time; keep your phone or clock out of your reach. This reduces the frustration of seeing how late it might be.

6. Maintain **STRICT SLEEPING AND WAKING TIMES**. Do not nap during the day. The aim is to be in bed for approximately 8 hours each night.

For a free DARE audio to help you sleep visit
www.DareResponse.com/Audios

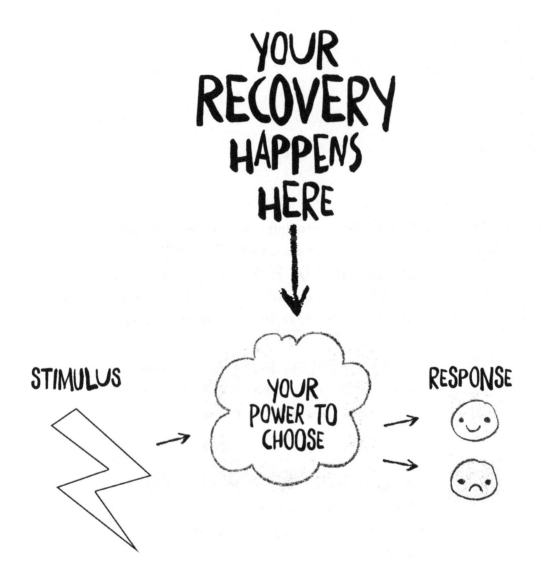

'BETWEEN STIMULUS AND RESPONSE THERE IS A SPACE. IN THAT SPACE IS OUR POWER TO CHOOSE OUR RESPONSE. IN OUR RESPONSE LIES OUR GROWTH AND OUR FREEDOM.'

VIKTOR FRANKL

WRITE A LETER TO YOUR ANXIETY MONSTER

TELL IT ABOUT THE
NEW AND IMPROVED
RELATIONSHIP YOU WANT
TO HAVE WITH IT.

YOU ARE YOUR OWN SAFE ZONE

YOU CAN RELY ON YOURSELF IN ANY SITUATION. YOUR BODY CAN HANDLE IT. YOU CAN HANDLE IT. YOU'RE ALL YOU NEED.

'I'M GOING TO
MAKE YOU SO
PROUD.'

NOTE TO SELF

LIST ALL THE CRUTCHES YOU USE TO FEEL SAFE.

1. ALWAYS HAVING MY PHONE WITH ME.
....

2. NEVER LEAVING HOME WITHOUT MY PARTNER.
....

....

....

....

....

....

....

SPEND A DAY WITHOUT YOUR MOST IMPORTANT CRUTCH. HOW DID IT GO?

....

....

....

....

....

....

....

....

....

USE THE
DARE APP TO HELP YOU
DO SOMETHING BRAVE

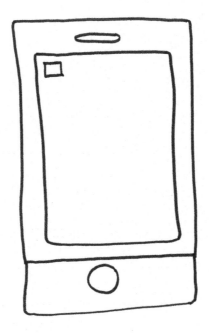

THE DARE APP IS AVAILABLE FOR BOTH IPHONE AND
ANDROID PHONES, WWW.DARERESPONSE.COM/WORKBOOK

THEN UPLOAD
THE PHOTO TO OUR DARE
FACEBOOK GROUP

(SEARCH 'DARE SUCCESS STORIES' ON FACEBOOK)

DO YOU WANT TO MAKE
A FAST RECOVERY?

IF SO,
ASK YOURSELF
THIS QUESTION
EVERYDAY...

'WHAT LEVEL OF ANXIOUS
DISCOMFORT AM I WILLING
TO EXPERIENCE IN ORDER TO
HEAL MY ANXIETY?'

'EVER TRIED.
EVER FAILED.
NO MATTER.
TRY AGAIN.
FAIL AGAIN.
FAIL BETTER.'

SAMUEL BECKETT

MICRO-BRAVERY

In order to win back the freedom that anxiety has stolen, you need to CONTINUALLY STEP OUTSIDE YOUR COMFORT ZONE and push into your fears.

So how do you face your fears when you feel overwhelmed? With 'micro-bravery'. Micro-bravery means FOCUSING ON AND ACCOMPLISHING THE SMALL CHALLENGES OF DAILY LIFE that will build up your confidence rather than only focusing on the really big challenges.

Taking small, everyday risks removes us from our personal comfort zones and challenges our fears. Bravery is built not born. It is a skill you develop through practice and consciously choosing to do things that slightly scare you.

Write down some examples of small steps that will help you overcome your anxiety.

For free DARE audios to help build confidence to face your challenges visit www.DareResponse.com/Audios

WRITE DOWN SOME EXAMPLES OF SMALL STEPS THAT WILL HELP YOU OVERCOME YOUR ANXIETY

....

....

....

....

....

....

....

....

....

....

....

HAVING AN ANXIETY
PROBLEM DOES NOT MAKE
YOU A COWARDLY PERSON,

YOU ARE
BRAVE BEYOND
BELIEF!

DARE TO EXERCISE

If you're looking for a 'Magic Pill' to elevate your mood and reduce feelings of anxiety or depression, exercise is the closest thing we currently have AND it comes with zero side effects! The mental benefits of exercise are:

☑ REDUCED ANXIETY

☑ IMPROVEMENT IN MOOD

☑ BETTER SLEEP

☑ PREVENT COGNITIVE DECLINE

☑ INCREASED ENERGY

☑ MORE SELF-CONFIDENCE.

EXERCISES YOU ENJOY

....

....

....

....

....

....

....

....

....

....

....

....

DRINK MORE WATER!

Dehydration contributes to anxiety and nervousness. The good news is that it is easily remedied by drinking more water daily. By drinking 8 GLASSES OF FRESH WATER SPREAD THROUGHOUT THE DAY you will notice a significant decrease in sensitization and anxious feelings. But these are many other benefits too. Water helps to:

- ☑ INCREASE ENERGY AND RELIEVE FATIGUE

- ☑ PROMOTE WEIGHT LOSS

- ☑ FLUSH OUT TOXINS

- ☑ IMPROVE SKIN COMPLEXION

- ☑ BOOST YOUR IMMUNE SYSTEM

- ☑ PREVENT CRAMPS AND SPRAINS

DON'T FORGET
TO STAY WELL
HYDRATED!

POWER POSE

Certain power poses can actually change your body chemistry!
Studies show that adopting a 'HIGH POWER POSE' like the ones
seen here FOR JUST 2 MINUTES can help drop your cortisol levels.
This helps you to feel much less anxious or afraid. Choose a power
pose and hold it for 2 minutes.

DO ONE OF THE FOLLOWING POWER POSES FOR 2 MINUTES

NOTICE HOW YOU FEEL BEFORE AND AFTER

STANDING WIDE STANCE

HANDS ON HIPS

ARMS RAISED ABOVE
HEAD IN A 'V'

ARMS CROSSED BEHIND
THE HEAD, SITTING OR
STANDING

MOOD PLAYLIST

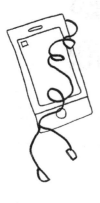

WRITE DOWN THE SONGS THAT MOTIVATE AND INSPIRE YOU

....

....

....

....

....

....

....

....

....

COURAGE BOARD
CREATE A COLLAGE OF iMAGES THAT WILL INSPIRE YOU ON ANXIOUS DAYS

*YOU CAN DO THIS ONLiNE WITH PINTEREST.

DE-STRESS IN NATURE

SPEND MORE TIME IN NATURE THIS WEEK.

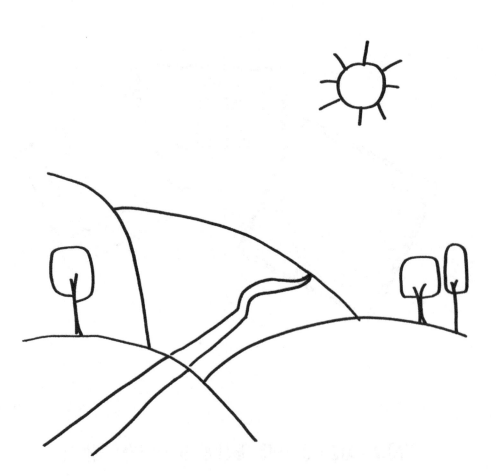

WHERE CAN YOU GO?
WHAT CAN YOU DO NEAR YOU?

....

....

....

....

....

....

....

....

....

....

....

....

RELEASE WORRY

WHAT ARE YOU WORRIED ABOUT RIGHT NOW? CAN YOU ACT ON IT, AND IF YES, WHAT CAN YOU DO?

....

....

....

WHAT IS OUTSIDE YOUR CONTROL? ARE YOU WILLING TO LET GO OF THESE WORRIES?

....

....

....

WORRY WINDOW

PLACE YOUR HAND HERE AND
ALLOW YOURSELF TO WORRY ABOUT
ANYTHING AT ALL FOR 5 MINUTES.
THEN STOP! YOU CAN
DO THIS JUST ONCE A DAY.

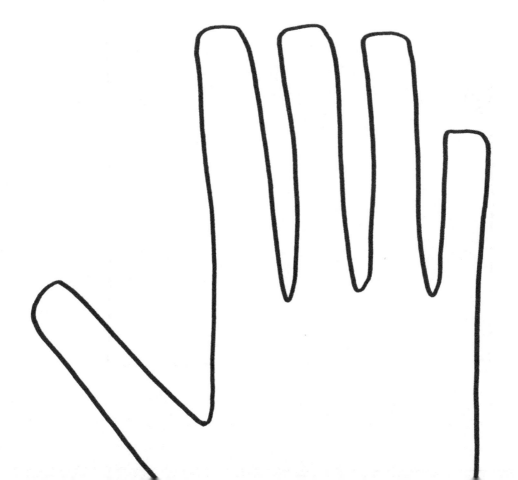

ENDING
HEALTH ANXIETY

WRITE YOUR MOST COMMON
HEALTH ANXIETIES HERE:

SIGN THIS BINDING AGREEMENT WITH YOURSELF:

FROM THIS DAY FORWARD, I AM NO LONGER GOING TO FEED MY HEALTH ANXIETIES. I WILL GET ANY HEALTH ISSUE I AM WORRIED ABOUT CHECKED OUT BUT AFTER THAT I WILL STOP SECOND GUESSING MY GOOD HEALTH. I AM NO LONGER GOING TO RUN TO GOOGLE TO RESEARCH EVERY NEW SENSATION I FEEL. I WILL STOP TORTURING MYSELF IN THIS WAY. LIFE IS TOO SHORT.

SIGN BELOW

_____

WRITE THE THINGS YOU WORRY ABOUT in THE BALLOONS

DRAW MORE BALLOONS IF YOU NEED THEM

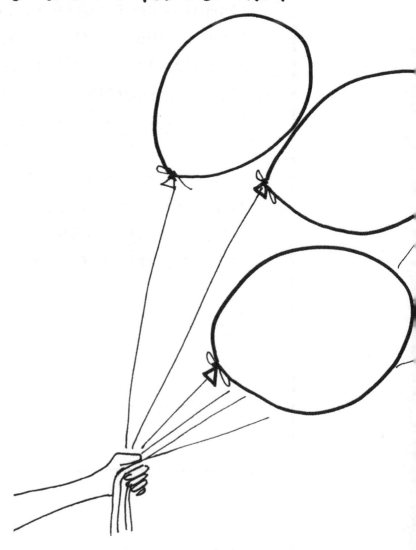

NOW: ARE YOU WILLING TO RELEASE THESE?

*CLOSE YOUR EYES AND IMAGINE THE BALLOONS
FLOATING AWAY

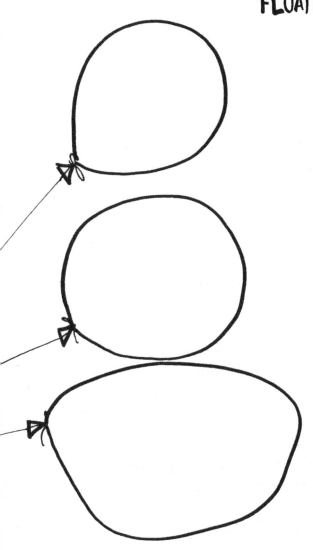

ENDiNG iNTRUSiVE THOUGHTS

It's perfectly normal to start fearing for your sanity or to get upset when intrusive thoughts manifest, but you must understand they're nothing more than the result of the ELEVATED STRESS HORMONES, MENTAL EXHAUSTION AND A CREATIVE IMAGINATION. The very fact that you're responding with anxiety to these thoughts proves that you're perfectly normal!

INTRUSiVE THOUGHTS = STRESS HORMONES + CREATiVE IMAGiNATiON + EXHAUSTiON

The harder you push those thoughts away from your mind, the harder they bounce back.

Remember as a child when you played with an inflatable beach ball in the sea? Every time you tried to push it down under the water to sit on it, it just kept springing back up with THE SAME FORCE YOU USED TO KEEP IT DOWN, often hitting you on the face. The same goes for these intrusive thoughts. You simply can't expect to escape or reduce them by pushing them away. The only way to get peace is to allow that BEACH BALL TO FLOAT ALONG BESIDE YOU.

Remember that YOU ARE NOT THESE THOUGHTS!

These INTRUSIVE THOUGHTS DO NOT REPRESENT THE REAL YOU. They're just a result of your creative, albeit overactive, imagination mixed with anxiety and exhaustion. In fact, rather than beat yourself up over them, you can congratulate yourself on your creative ability! With practice you can learn to have intrusive thoughts without any fearful reaction to them. When there is no fearful reaction, the thoughts become less and less frequent until they no longer appear.

ALLOW THE BEACH BALL TO FLOAT ALONG

ANXIOUS
OR INTRUSIVE
THOUGHTS END
WHEN YOU **LOWER**
YOUR GENERAL
ANXIETY LEVEL

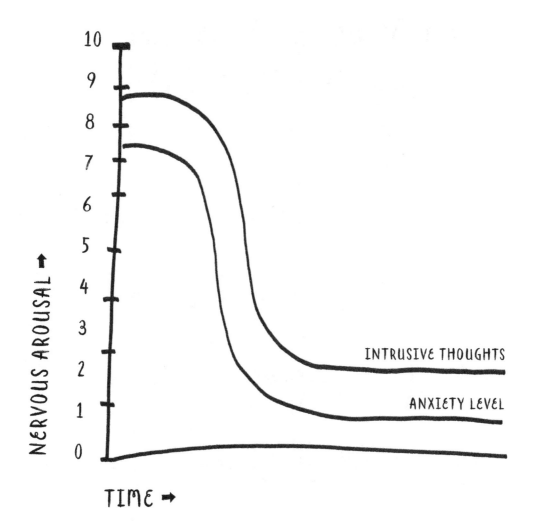

ANXIETY CAN ALSO
MAKE YOU FEEL WEiRDLY
DiSCONNECTED FROM LIFE
(DEPERSONALIZATION)

BUT
ONCE YOUR ANXIETY LEVELS COME DOWN, THIS STRANGE SENSATION WILL END

DON'T BUY INTO LABELS

People tend to over-identify with mental health labels once they have been given one by a person with authority (For example, a doctor or psychologist). DO NOT ALLOW YOURSELF TO BE DEFINED BY A LABEL. You are not your anxiety. As abnormal as it makes you feel, this anxiety is not the real you. It is not who you are or who you have become.

Once your anxiety level starts to drop and the stress hormones are slowly flushed from your system, you'll start to feel a whole lot more like your old confident self again. ANXIETY IS A TEMPORARY PROBLEM. Do not let it define who you really are or who you might become.

DON'T LET YOURSELF BE DEFINED BY A LABEL

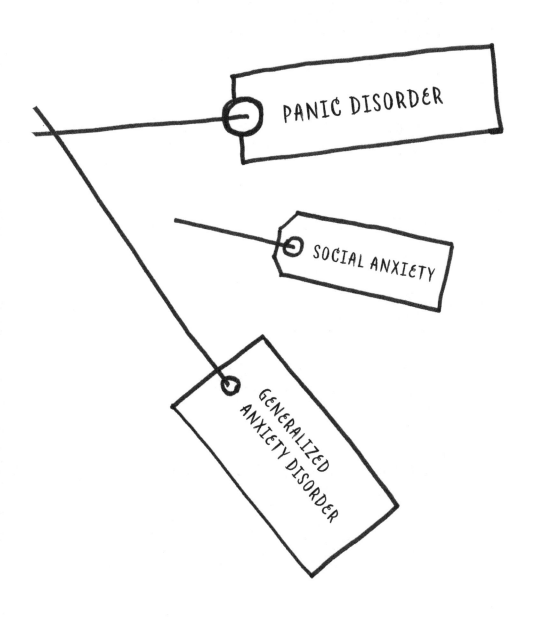

LAUGH IT OFF!
MAKE A LIST OF ALL THE FUNNY MOVIES YOU LOVE

GROUNDHOG DAY
....

....

....

....

....

....

....

....

WHEN WAS THE LAST TIME YOU HAD A GOOD BELLY LAUGH?

....
....
....
....
....
....
....
....
....
....

DO MORE OF THIS.

WRITE YOUR FAVOURITE QUOTE HERE:

WRITE YOUR
FAVOURITE DARE
QUOTE HERE:

WHAT WOULD YOU
LiKE A FRIEND OR YOUR
PARTNER TO SAY TO
YOU WHEN YOU FEEL
VERY ANXiOUS?

WRITE IT IN THE BOX
ON THE OPPOSITE PAGE,
CUT IT OUT AND GIVE IT
TO THEM.

REPEAT THESE AFFIRMATIONS TO WIRE IN YOUR NEW DARING MINDSET.

I AM SAFE.

I CAN HANDLE THIS.

I ACCEPT AND ALLOW THIS ANXIOUS FEELING.

I AM MY OWN SAFE PERSON.

THIS TOO SHALL PASS.

I AM THE CURE.

I AM A WARRIOR.

IT'S JUST THOUGHTS, JUST SENSATIONS.

I AM COMFORTABLE WITH THIS ANXIOUS DISCOMFORT.

I AM EXCITED BY THIS FEELING.

BRING IT ON!

I WILL NOT GIVE UP.

I ACCEPT AND ALLOW THIS ANXIOUS THOUGHT.

I AM MY OWN SAFE ZONE.

I WILL NOT GIVE IN.

I AM MY OWN COMFORT ZONE.

I GROW STRONGER BECAUSE OF THIS.

EVERYTHING I WANT IS ON THE OTHER SIDE OF FEAR.

I AM RELEASING RESISTANCE.

I WILL NOT LET ANXIETY STEAL MY FREEDOM.

I AM RELEASING FEAR.

I AM WINNING BACK FREEDOM.

SENSATIONS ARE JUST SENSATIONS.

I KNOW THE GIFT IS IN THE WOUND.

I CAN STAY HERE AS LONG AS NECESSARY.

THOUGHT ARE JUST THOUGHTS.

I AM IN A STATE OF FLOW.

FEAR IS JUST A FEELING.

I'VE GOT THIS.

I AM RELEASING TENSION.

I AM THE MASTER OF MY FATE.

ANXIETY IS NOT A WEAKNESS.

I DO NOT NEED TO RUN.

I AM THE HUNTER NOT THE HUNTED.

THE ONLY WAY OUT IS THROUGH.

I HAVE SURVIVED 100% OF MY PANIC ATTACKS TO DATE.

I AM NOT MY ANXIETY.

I AM SAFE NO MATTER WHERE I AM.

I DO NOT FIGHT THIS FEELING.

I DO NOT RESIST ANYMORE.

I FEEL IT, I EMBRACE IT. I ALLOW IT.

I AM STRONG.

I AM MORE THAN ENOUGH.

EVERYTHING I NEED IS INSIDE OF ME.

SETBACKS ARE PART OF THE RECOVERY.

IT IS ALWAYS DARKEST BEFORE THE DAWN.

I AM THE CURE.

GIVE
YOURSELF THE
GIFT OF DEEP
RELAXATION

DOWNLOAD THE FREE
DARE AUDIOS AT:

WWW.DARERESPONSE.COM/AUDIOS

Part 4

THE HOME STRETCH

→

In this 4th and final part, you will
learn how to move beyond setbacks
and thinking of yourself as an 'anxious
person', to seeing yourself in a BOLD
AND BRAVE NEW LIGHT.

Part 4
THE
HOME
STRETCH

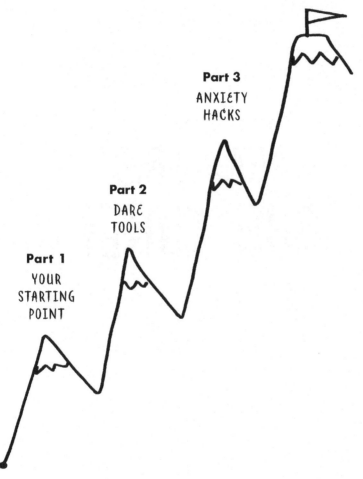

Part 3
ANXIETY
HACKS

Part 2
DARE
TOOLS

Part 1
YOUR
STARTING
POINT

YOU ARE
THE CURE!

NO ONE SAVES
US BUT OURSELVES.
NO ONE CAN
AND NO ONE MAY.
WE OURSELVES MUST
WALK THE PATH.

BUDDHA

RECOVERY IS NOT
A LINEAR PROCESS
LiKE THIS

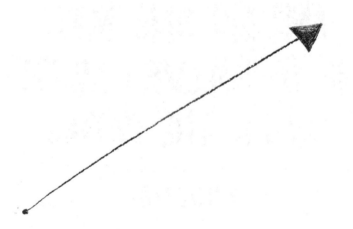

IT'S MORE
LIKE THIS

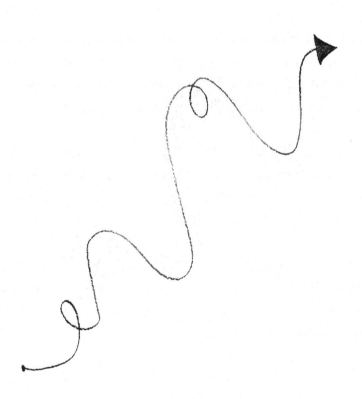

SETBACKS!

It's almost GUARANTEED THAT YOU'LL HAVE A MAJOR SETBACK during your recovery. Setbacks are like final-stage exams you have to pass in order to earn your freedom.

Setbacks are particularly common after you've had a significant breakthrough, such as doing something that you were previously anxious about, e.g., overcoming a major obstacle or after a significant life event such as moving or changing jobs.

Recovery is NOT A LINEAR PROCESS like healing a broken bone. Some days will be better than others—that's just the way it is, so don't get upset if you complete something successfully one day but fail the next.

Since setbacks are almost a guarantee, you should expect them and welcome them! If you fully understand that setbacks are part of the healing process, you can drop the frustration you feel and move through them with greater speed.

WRITE A **SHORT ENCOURAGING LETTER** TO YOURSELF THAT YOU CAN READ WHENEVER YOU ARE DEALING WITH A SETBACK

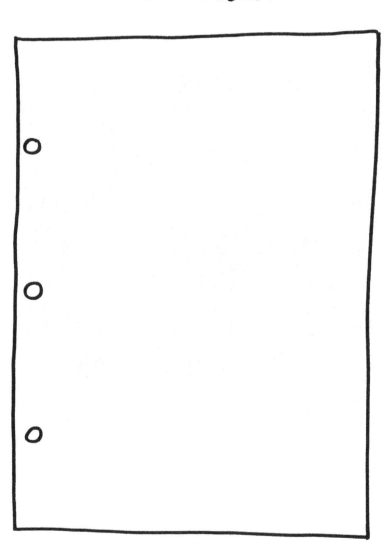

NEVER COMPARE
THE SPEED OF YOUR
RECOVERY TO OTHERS.

THE JOURNEY OF
RECOVERY IS DONE AT EACH
INDIVIDUAL'S OWN SPEED.
DON'T COMPARE YOURSELF
TO OTHERS, YOU DO NOT
KNOW THEIR HISTORY.
ALLOW YOURSELF TO HEAL
IN YOUR OWN TIME.

'COMPARISON
iS THE THIEF
OF JOY.'

THEODORE ROOSEVELT

WHEN YOU FACE YOUR ANXIETY WITH DARE, YOU WILL EXPERIENCE SOME RESISTANCE

WHAT RESISTANCE HAVE YOU NOTICED COMING UP?

1. NOT WANTING TO PRACTICE.

2. THINKING MY ANXIETY IS DIFFERENT (MORE STUBBORN).

EXCUSES YOUR
ANXIOUS MIND MIGHT
CREATE TO STOP YOU
FROM DARING.

PEOPLE WHO SUFFER FROM ANXIETY ARE ORDINARY HEROES

THEY GET UP EACH DAY AND GET ON WITH LIFE, PICKING THEMSELVES UP AFTER EACH AND EVERY SETBACK. IT DOES NOT MAKE HEADLINE NEWS BUT IT COUNTS BECAUSE IT IS REAL BRAVERY, TRUE COURAGE.

DRAW YOUR
DARE SUPERHERO
SLOGAN HERE

'LIFE SHRINKS
OR EXPANDS IN
PROPORTION TO ONE'S
COURAGE.'

ANAIS NIN

KEEP A
WINNING MINDSET
BY USING THE FREE
'MOTIVATIONAL AND
SUCCESS' DARE AUDIOS
FOUND AT:
WWW.DARERESPONSE.
COM/AUDIOS

KNOW THE
WARNING SIGNS

WHAT ARE THE SIGNS THAT ANXIETY is CREEPING BACK INTO YOUR LIFE?

EARLY WARNINGS	STEPS TO TAKE
MORNING ANXIETY	DAILY WELLNESS ROUTINE
ANXIOUS THOUGHTS	RE-READ DARE FOR INTRUSIVE THOUGHTS

YOUR **VERY BEST FRIEND** TELLS YOU THEY HAVE A SIMILAR ANXIETY PROBLEM AS YOU. WRITE THEM A LETTER OF ADVICE.

DEAR BFF,

WHAT BIG CHALLENGES HAVE YOU ALREADY OVERCOME IN YOUR LIFE?

WHAT DID YOU LEARN FROM THOSE EXPERIENCES?

....

....

....

....

....

....

....

....

....

....

SELF CARE

Developing a sense of compassion for yourself and your struggle with anxiety speeds up your recovery time.

Imagine if your best friend or someone you care about was struggling with anxiety in the exact same manner as you. Take a moment to FEEL A DEEP SENSE OF EMPATHY FOR THEM and their struggle. Now think about your own struggle with anxiety. How you have battled so hard alone. Think about your first panic attack or all those nights you felt so lost and alone.

Now turn that same empathy you felt for your friend towards yourself. SUPPORT YOURSELF in the same way you would your best friend.

Don't try to find a reason to justify your love. Instead, give your love to yourself unconditionally and without reserve. You don't need a reason, and you don't need anyone to say you deserve it. Choose to love yourself unapologetically.

IF YOU HAD A TIME MACHINE AND COULD GO BACK TO WHEN ANXIETY FIRST BECAME A PROBLEM, WHAT WOULD YOU TELL YOURSELF?

....

....

....

....

....

....

....

....

....

....

WHAT ADVICE WOULD
THE HAPPIEST VERSION
OF YOUR 80 YEAR OLD SELF
GIVE TO YOU?

'EVERYTHING IS DANGEROUS, MY DEAR FELLOW. IF IT WASN'T SO, LIFE WOULDN'T BE WORTH LIVING.'

OSCAR WILDE

DARE
CHALLENGE
MAP

MAP KEY

List your Challenges Here

🚙 DRIVING

....

🍴 EATING OUT

....

....

....

....

....

DRAW YOUR CHALLENGES ONTO THE MAP.

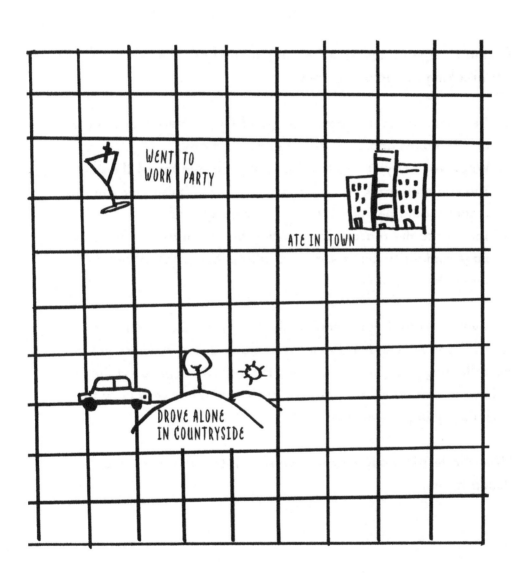

THE X-EFFECT

Lasting change comes from creating healthy new habits
(Or breaking old unhealthy ones).

1. Get some paper and draw a copy of the X-effect chart. There
    are 49 boxes and each box represents a day.
2. When you set yourself a habit, enter it at the top of the page.
    You can only track one habit per sheet. The habit you want to
    create should be very specific and measurable.
3. Then write the reasons for creating this habit at the top of the
    page and write the reward you will give yourself once you
    reach the 49th day.

For every day that you complete the task you add an X to the
chart. If you miss a day you leave it blank and make sure you do it
the following day. Once you reach the end (49 days later) the new
behaviour will be wired into your brain making it very easy to do
each day going forward.

*(The X-effect is a hugely successful habit tool that started on a
Reddit forum)

HABIT: ....

REASONS: ....

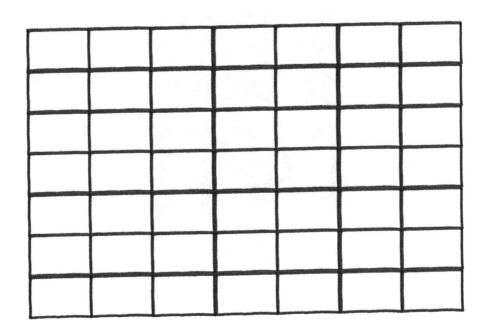

REWARD: ....

BE BOLD,
BE BRAVE,
DARE!

FOLLOW THE DAILY WELLNESS
ROUTINE AND SET YOURSELF A
DARING CHALLENGE EACH DAY

TRACK YOUR PROGRESS
ON THE FOLLOWING PAGES

YOU CAN PRINT MORE SHEETS OFF AT:
WWW.DARERESPONSE.COM/SHEETS.

SAMPLE DARE DAILY CHALLENGE SHEET

DATE: MAY 9TH

LOCATION: CAR

MOOD BEFORE:

DESCRIBE MOOD: SCARED

MOOD AFTER:

DESCRIBE MOOD: CONFIDENT

TODAY I DARED TO:

I DROVE WELL OUTSIDE MY COMFORT ZONE AND SAT IN BUMPER TO BUMPER TRAFFIC FOR AN HOUR! YIPEE!!

WHAT I LEARNED FROM THIS CHALLENGE:

THAT AFTER THE FIRST WAVE OF ANXIETY PASSED, THE SENSATIONS SUBSIDED. I COULD HAVE STAYED THERE ALL DAY!

WHERE DO YOU FEEL ANXIOUS?

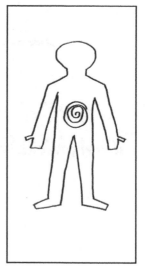

*You can print more sheets off at: www.dareresponse.com/sheets

DARE DAILY
CHALLENGE SHEET

DATE: ....   LOCATION: ....

MOOD BEFORE:

☺ 😐 ☹

DESCRIBE MOOD: ....

MOOD AFTER:

☺ 😐 ☹

DESCRIBE MOOD: ....

TODAY I DARED TO:

....
....
....
....

WHERE DO YOU FEEL ANXIOUS?

WHAT I LEARNED FROM
THIS CHALLENGE:

....
....
....
....

DARE WEEKLY PROGRESS SAMPLE

WEEK: 1ST MAY

	WELLNESS ROUTINE	DARE CHALLENGE COMPLETED	ANXIETY LEVEL 1-10 (HIGH)
MONDAY	✓	✓	7
TUESDAY	✓	✓	6
WEDNESDAY	✓	✓	7
THURSDAY	✓	✓	8
FRIDAY	✓	✓	3
SATURDAY	✓	✓	3
SUNDAY	✓	✓	3

NOTES/INSIGHTS:

I DID REALLY WELL THIS WEEK. I PUSHED OUTSIDE MY COMFORT ZONE AND STARTED TO REALLY SEE THROUGH THE ILLUSION MY ANXIETY CREATES. BRING ON THE NEXT WEEK!

DARE WEEKLY PROGRESS SHEET

WEEK: ....

	WELLNESS ROUTINE	DARE CHALLENGE COMPLETED	ANXIETY LEVEL 1-10 (HIGH)
MONDAY	☐	☐	☐
TUESDAY	☐	☐	☐
WEDNESDAY	☐	☐	☐
THURSDAY	☐	☐	☐
FRIDAY	☐	☐	☐
SATURDAY	☐	☐	☐
SUNDAY	☐	☐	☐

NOTES/INSIGHTS:

....

....

....

NEVER

GiVE UP!

THIS WORKBOOK IS BASED ON THE BEST SELLING BOOK DARE. HERE ARE WORDS OF ENCOURAGEMENT FROM THE DARE COMMUNITY:

'DARE will teach you that anxiety is your protector, and its only job is to keep you safe...never to harm you. Sometimes it is simply overprotective. DARE will teach you to take anxiety by the hand, befriend it and show it you are safe. 'What you resist persists, and what you accept you can transform.' KELLY

''Know that the fear you are feeling, if reversed, can transform you into the bravest person ever!! You are strong, you are brave and you control you!! DARE ON!!!' NICOLE

'Just remember that this is not a straight path. There will be ups and downs. There will be days you doubt whether the program is even working. These are the moments it's crucial to keep trusting in the program and in your bodies ability to handle whatever anxiety throws your way. You are so much stronger than you can even begin to imagine. Keep moving forward. One step at a time , one day at a time. And give time the time it needs. It's all worth it!' TRACY

'I was skeptical this would work because DARE was completely different from everything else I had read. Once I understood and practiced the steps, I couldn't believe how simple it actually is.' BRAD

'The journey is long,hard and requires determination, but the strong happy person you become after you get through this is beyond your wildest dreams! Don't ever give up!' SUZANE

'You are not alone, anxiety comes in many forms, and it will not kill you or send you crazy, you are perfectly safe and you will get better, you are going to be ok, this is not forever. Use DARE and talk to others in this program, you are not the only one suffering with these wild anxiety symptoms. You will get through this. God bless you, you are so brave xx' GAYLE

'How long will it take me to recover?' Do your best to let go of this question, and just do the DARE steps one day at a time. Even if your full recovery is months away, you'll find yourself feeling better and better, able to do more and more, as you keep practicing your DARE skills. However long it takes you to recover, it's just a short time compared to the lifetime of freedom that awaits you. You WILL succeed!' LAURA

'Whether you like it or not, you've been practicing this habit of being afraid of feeling fearful for so long. Don't be so hard on yourself because you've been doing the best you can. Believe that you CAN do this because getting your life back is worth everything! Remember: It's not about being fearLESS but rather being BRAVE in the face of fear.' NINA

'Rather than being afraid of the fear and anxiety, DARE has taught me to embrace those feelings and turn them into a fire that propels me to do more than I have ever done. Comfortable in the uncomfortable has meant that nothing can stop me now. It's me and the world.' ZANIA

'A thought is just a thought. A sensation is just a sensation. They only get bigger and scarier when you allow your squirrel brain (amygdala) to get hijacked. Accept it all without placing meaning or judgement to it. Change all the scary 'what ifs' with a positive... 'what if this really works?' (It does by the way) Go ahead, I triple dog DARE you!' CRYSTAL

'I paid for psychiatry, group therapy, and bought many books and audio tapes for approximately 35 years. Nothing escalated my success over anxiety like the book DARE has done for me. It changed my life.' SUZANNE

'No matter where your thoughts take you we have all been there. With lots of hard work I got through and you will to! DARE.' CONNIE

'Fake it till you make it, the mind believes what you tell it. Small steps lead to giant leaps. Be kind to yourself. You are the cure, you got this.' SUSAN

'DARE works if you truly give your all to the whole program. You are NOT too old; too severe a case; or too unique for this not to be successful #darebfree.' MICHAELA

'Now You probably feel like you're down in the dumps and you're all alone but I promise there is light at the end of the tunnel and the experience you are going through will only make you stronger.' BRIGETTE

'You can never go back to where you were because you know too much now you know what it is and you know it can't hurt you.' DUNS

'Once you will get better and you will get better fear in everyday life will become like a walk in the park! Guaranteed.' JACKOB

'You don't need to live like this. It's time to trust yourself and begin your DARE journey. It works!!' KELLY

'I've had Agoraphobia for 26 years (since I was 18) and have never found anything which helped me until DARE. I finally feel hope for the first time, that this doesn't need to be my life forever. These techniques DO work if you work with them.' LISA

'DARE to be the best, anxiety free, version of yourself. Do it today and live the life you want, the life you deserve!' KYLA

'I know what I needed to hear, that I never did, 'there is nothing, and no symptom you feel, that is new. As bad as it can feel, millions of others have felt it and are perfectly fine.' DANIEL

'Remember, Setbacks are just a setup for a great comeback! Keep forcing yourself into those uncomfortable situations, it IS the key to recovery!' CRISTAN

'In my many years working in both mainstream and alternative therapeutic environments DARE is the the best approach I have come across for healing anxiety yes, healing, not merely 'managing' - bar none. It has helped, and continues to help me personally, as well as the people I know who also experience anxiety and who I have recommended the book to. DARE is a true classic in the world of self-help books and will stand the test of time. Just get started, and then keep going - you won't regret it and will be setting yourself up for life.' SHYRON

'Accept and allow your fears by remembering they are only exaggerated feelings, face them and let them be, they cannot hurt you.' SANDRA

'DARE = a way to heal anxiety by acceptance and love. Welcome to the DARE family. You are not alone.' MALIN

'I now remember what it's like to live in the moment and enjoy life the way God intended.' IRENE

'Everything you want is on the other side of fear. Befriend the fear, love the fear and then you will be free from the fear. You are not alone, we are all doing this together.'VICKY

'We are warriors and warriors never have to fight alone! Together we can beat this thing called 'anxiety' with the DARE steps that are given to us!' HEATHER

'In the words of Gene Kranz from Apollo 13, 'Failure is not an option!' MARINA

'Never give in and never give up. I promise better days are coming if you feed your anxiety with DARE 100%.' KRISTAN

'You are not alone. You are strong and you are enough. You can do this!' JULI

'Push on and never give up. Anxiety steals so much from us. Start reclaiming it back. Make your life what you want it to be. Write your story. Don't let anxiety write it for you. Dare on.' LUCY

'Even when you think you can't, you CAN. Do the DARE work one hour at a time and you will see.' IDA

'The greatest lesson is to become your own hero through your gifts that anxiety will give you as they unfold on the journey through dare.'SPATARO

'Stick with it! DARE completely contradicts everything you have ever tried before to manage anxiety, but that is the reason it works. It is difficult at first and you may feel hesitant or nervous about these counterintuitive strategies, but it doesn't take long to realise why DARE has been so successful for so many people.' JESSICA

'The cure is within you. DARE will help you find it.' SHERRI

'The ONLY way out is through and I guarantee you are strong enough to DARE through it to a far happier life on the other side. You've got this!' LILA

'Know that you are your own safe zone! You will win over anxiety! Trust and believe in the DARE process. You have a life to live!' COLLEEN

'We can be our best and worst enemy. The power this program gives, is not only to show you that you are the cure for yourself but you have the dare army behind you! You're never alone.' GEORGIA-RAE

'It is a process, there may be tears, bumps, frustration..but remember you have this. Anxiety is a liar and you need to stand up to that 'bully' and say no more. Do your worst! Never lose hope and always keep believing in you ...' SIOBHÁN

'Be glad that you've had this experience, one day you will look back & see how much you have grown & your life will be enriched.' WENDY

'Dare is the key to the lock on the door of freedom.' SAMANTHA

'You only get one life, get out there and live it. Anxiety is a lie so go enjoy life while you can.' LISA

'The beginning for me was more difficult than I could imagine. Some days I would really lose hope because the feelings were so intense and powerful. Don't give up no matter how bad or uncomfortable you feel. Things will get better, I promise!' JACKSON

'You have to give time...time. DARE works but it takes time and experiences to get where you want to be. Be present, love yourself and others.' THERESE

'Trust the DARE process and quit making excuses. Be persistent but patient. NOW is the time to enjoy life again.' LEO ADAM

'Learn to replace fighting with accepting, running away from to running towards, wishing it away to demanding more and you will soon realise you had the key to freedom right there all the time. Dare to be free.' LORI

'Don't take life to seriously, it's not like your going to outlive it. Best of luck with new venture. My life is on the right track because of you and the dare team Xx.' KELLY

'Remember that you don't have to figure out everything at once. Take your time, do baby steps and the results will come!' SIMONA

'What you fear the most go and do it, and prove to anxiety you are in control, go and enjoy life and everything it offers, because life is worth enjoying.' JAYNE

'Leave the past where it belongs. You have the best anxiety toolkit now, so just get out there and get practicing! Short term discomfort = long term happiness. What have you got to lose!!' JENNIFER

'Dare works! But you have got to DARE you have to work hard and be patient. Trust the process.' LISA

'Believe in the process. When you get a setback (I'm sorry but you will get them) start over again by applying DARE. Apply every step and you will find that you have come a long way.' MALIN

'Don't worry about setbacks. They will come but you WILL get through them and be stronger for it. Slowly over time you'll find a shift in your thought process and life won't seem so daunting! Believe in yourself and DARE!' MICHELLE

'Trust in the DARE process. Healing is not linear. Expect good days and bad, even a few major setbacks. Practice, practice, practice--you are worth it!' NANCY

'Expect good days and bad days. It's all part of the journey. Give yourself lots of praise for even the smallest things you are able to do. Everything you do whether it's successful or unsuccessful builds upon the other. Before you know it, you are achieving goals you never thought imaginable.' SUZANNE

SEARCH 'DARE SUCCESS STORIES' ON FACEBOOK TO JOIN THIS GROUP OF AMAZING PEOPLE

SPECIAL THANKS!

Thank you to Tatyana Feeney for the illustrated design of this workbook. Graham Thew for the great book layout design and Sophia McDonagh (aka ye little skipper) for her important input on the time machine. Thank you also to Suzane Brikassa and John Quirke for proofreading the workbook. Lastly a special thanks to all the wonderful members of the DARE community who contribute in so many different and inspiring ways to help more and more people overcome their anxiety.

SPREAD THE WORD

I would love if you could LEAVE AN HONEST REVIEW ON AMAZON. It can be as short or as long as you like. Write whatever is true for you and your experience with this workbook. Your review will speak to the people who experience anxiety in the same way as you do.

Your message could help reach someone who's suffering in silence right now.

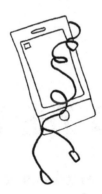

For Coaching, Bootcamps, the
DARE App and much, much more visit:

WWW.DARERESPONSE.COM